PIANO • VOCAL • GUITAR

TOP CHRISTIAN
2020-2021

ISBN 978-1-70513-346-0

HAL•LEONARD®

7777 W. BLUEMOUND RD. P.O. BOX 13819 MILWAUKEE, WI 53213

Visit Hal Leonard Online at
www.halleonard.com

Contact us:
Hal Leonard
7777 West Bluemound Road
Milwaukee, WI 53213
Email: info@halleonard.com

In Europe, contact:
Hal Leonard Europe Limited
42 Wigmore Street
Marylebone, London, W1U 2RN
Email: info@halleonardeurope.com

In Australia, contact:
Hal Leonard Australia Pty. Ltd.
4 Lentara Court
Cheltenham, Victoria, 3192 Australia
Email: info@halleonard.com.au

MW00783162

ALIVE & BREATHING

Words and Music by MATT MAHER
and ELLE LIMEBEAR

* Recorded a half step lower.

THE BLESSING

Words and Music by KARI JOBE CARNES,
CODY CARNES, STEVEN FURTICK
and CHRIS BROWN

Moderately

mf

* *Recorded a half step lower.*

GRAVES INTO GARDENS

Words and Music by CHRIS BROWN,
STEVEN FURTICK, TIFFANY HAMMER
and BRANDON LAKE

*Recorded a half step lower.

FAMOUS FOR
(I Believe)

Words and Music by TAUREN WELLS,
ALEXIS SLIFER, CHUCK BUTLER,
KRISSY NORDHOFF and JORDAN SAPP

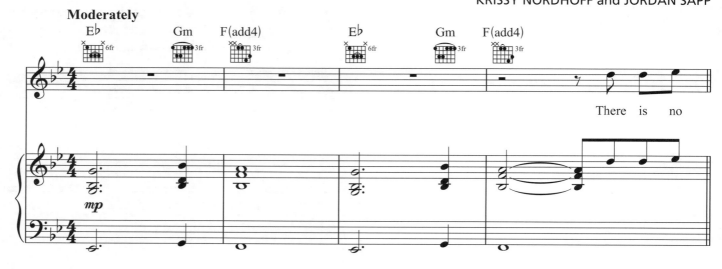

GOD SO LOVED

Words and Music by ED CASH,
SCOTT CASH, MARTIN CASH,
FRANNI CASH and ANDREW BERGTHOLD

God so loved the world that __ He gave us __ His one and on - ly Son to save us. __ Who-

ev - er __ be - lieves in __ Him __ will live for - ev - er. ___

GREAT THINGS

Words and Music by JONAS MYRIN
and PHIL WICKHAM

Recorded a half step lower.

I WILL FEAR NO MORE

Words and Music by JASON INGRAM,
MATT FUQUA, JOSHUA HAVENS,
DAN OSTEBO and JORDAN MOHILOWSKI

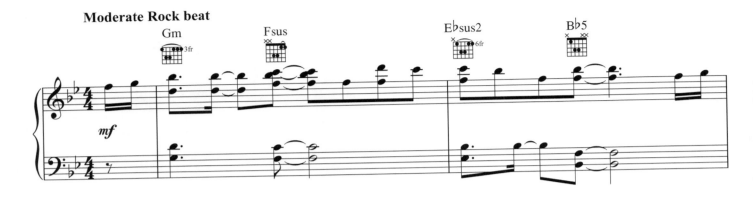

an - xious thought that steals my breath, it's a
lift my eyes, I will lift my cares, lay them

INTO THE SEA
(It's Gonna Be Ok)

Words and Music by BRYAN FOWLER,
MICAH KUIPER, TASHA LAYTON
and KEITH EVERETT SMITH

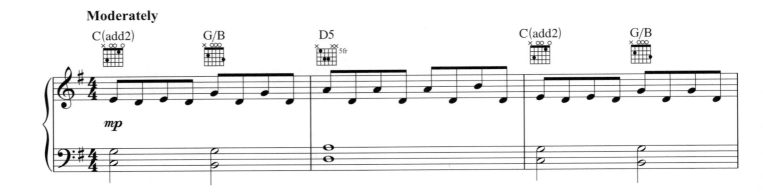

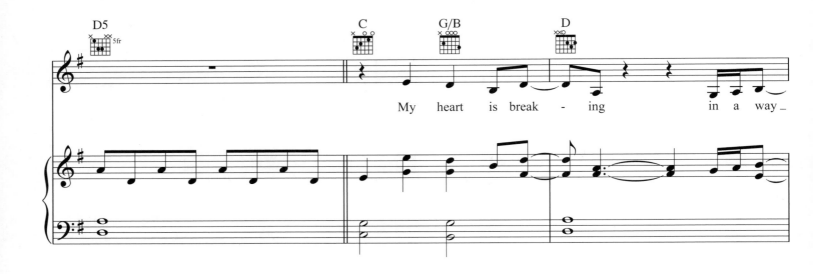

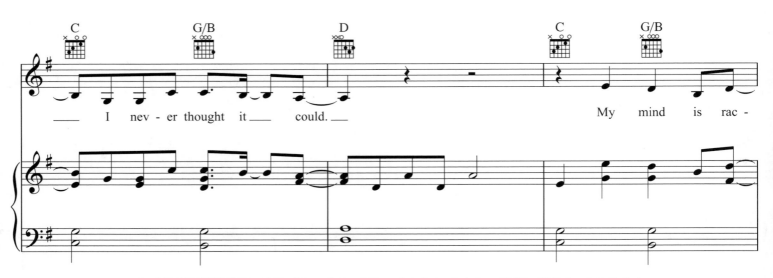

51

HOLD ON TO ME

Words and Music by LAUREN DAIGLE,
PAUL DUNCAN and PAUL MABURY

LOVE MOVED FIRST

Words and Music by MARK HALL,
MATTHEW WEST and BERNIE HERMS

PEACE BE STILL

Words and Music by MIA FIELDES,
ANDREW HOLT and HOPE DARST

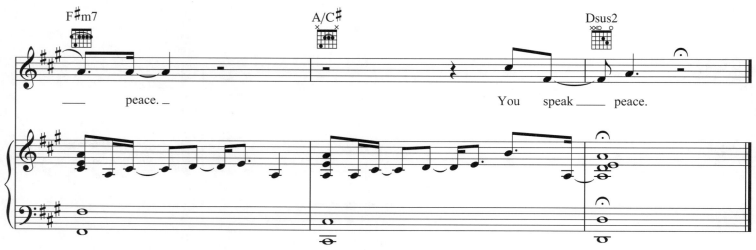

MAN OF YOUR WORD

Words and Music by CHANDLER MOORE,
NATHAN JESS, ANTHONY BROWN
and JONATHAN JAY

Moderate Gospel feel

All things are pos-si-ble when we be-lieve.

Old chains are break-a-ble when we re-ceive. Yah-weh, You keep Your

prom - is - es. ___ If You said ___ it, we be-lieve ___ it.

cresc.

* *Recorded a half step lower.*

SAY I WON'T

Words and Music by BART MILLARD
and JORDAN MOHILOWSKI

SEE A VICTORY

Words and Music by CHRIS BROWN,
STEVEN FURTICK, JASON INGRAM
and BEN FIELDING

The weap-on may __ be formed, __ but it ___ won't pros-

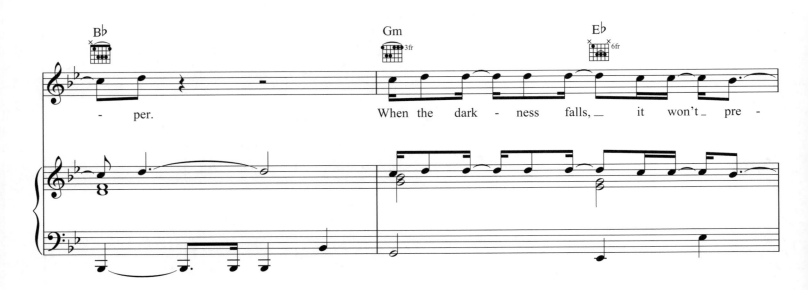

-per. When the dark-ness falls, __ it won't __ pre-

Gm   E♭

vic - to - ry,   I'm gon-na see a   vic - to - ry,   for the bat -

B♭   F   N.C.

- tle be - longs __ to You, Lord. _____   I'm gon - na see a

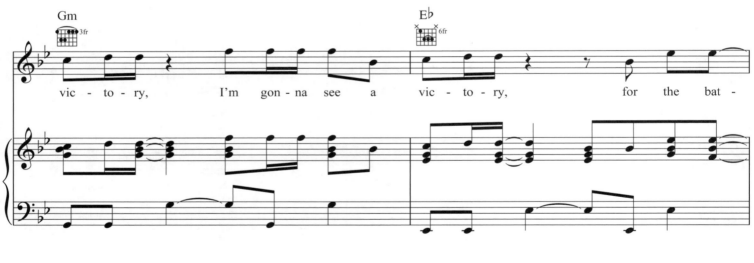

Gm   E♭

vic - to - ry,   I'm gon - na see a   vic - to - ry,   for the bat -

B♭   F

- tle be - longs __ to You, Lord. __   I'm gon - na see a

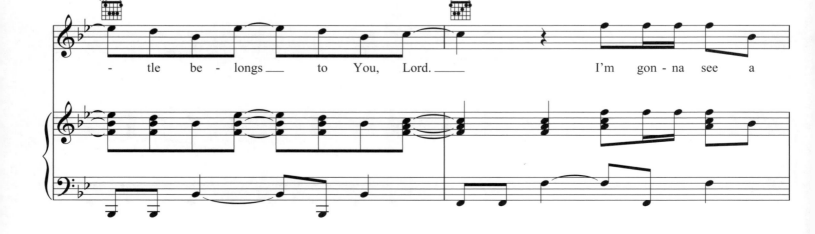

RISE UP
(Lazarus)

Words and Music by MADISON CAIN,
LOGAN CAIN, TAYLOR CAIN,
ETHAN HULSE and NICK SCHWARZ

STILL ROLLING STONES

Words and Music by LAUREN DAIGLE,
PAUL DUNCAN, JASON INGRAM
and PAUL MABURY

You're still roll-ing, roll-ing. ___ You're still roll-ing stones. ___

Much slower, freely

THERE WAS JESUS

Words and Music by CASEY BEATHARD,
JONATHAN SMITH and ZACH WILLIAMS

Country Ballad, in 2

Ev - 'ry time ___ I tried ___ to make ___ it on ___ my ___
___ I built ___ came crash - ing to ___ the ___

___ own, ___ ev - 'ry time ___ I tried ___ to stand ___
___ ground, when the friends ___ I had ___ were no -

___ and start ___ to ___ fall, and all those lone -
- where to ___ be ___ found, I could - n't see ___

D♭
A♭
4fr
- ing and the hurt - ing, like a bless - ing bur - ied in
E♭
3fr
the bro - ken piec - es. Ev - 'ry min -
Fm
D♭
- ute, ev - 'ry mo - ment, where I've been or where I'm go -
A♭
4fr
E♭
3fr
To Coda
- ing, e - ven when I did - n't know it, or could - n't see it,

TRUTH BE TOLD

Words and Music by ANDREW PRIUS
and MATTHEW WEST

Moderately slow

Lie num-ber one: you're sup-posed to have it all to-geth-er. And when they

ask, "How ya do-in'?" just smile_ and tell 'em, "Nev-er bet-ter."

Lie num-ber two: ev-'ry-bod-y's life is per-fect ex-cept ___ yours. So, keep your

*Recorded a half step lower.

122

WHO YOU ARE TO ME

Words and Music by HILLARY SCOTT,
CHARLES KELLEY, DAVE HAYWOOD
and CHRIS TOMLIN

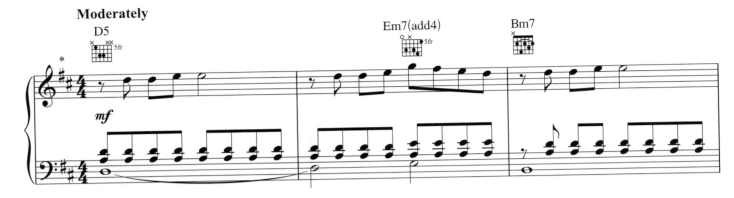

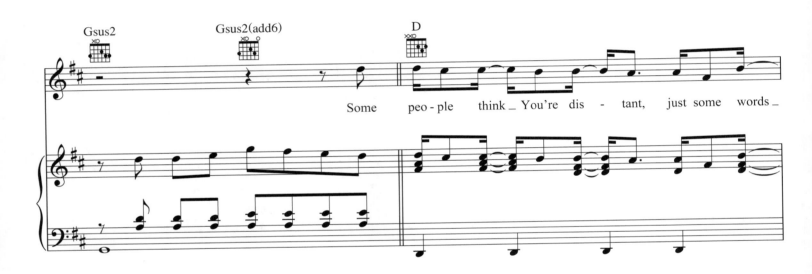

Some peo-ple think _ You're dis - tant, just some words _

_ on _ a page, _ that You're noth-ing more _ than fa - bles hand - ed down _

* *Recorded a half step lower.*

YOU KEEP HOPE ALIVE

Words and Music by JON REDDICK,
JESS CATES and ANTHONY SKINNER

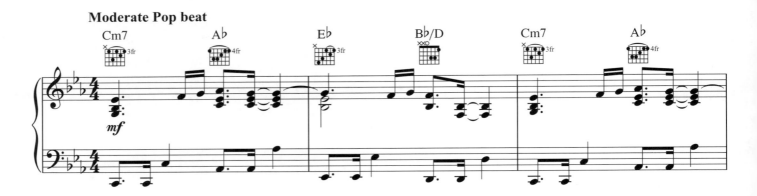

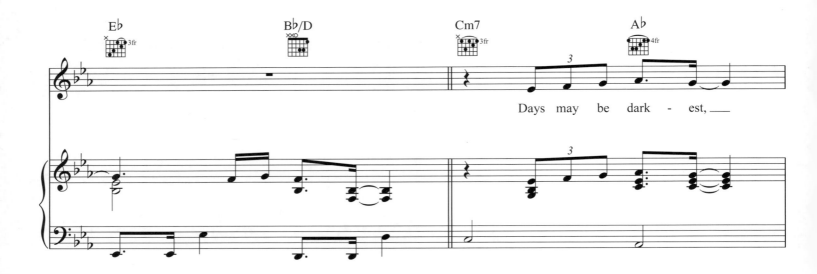

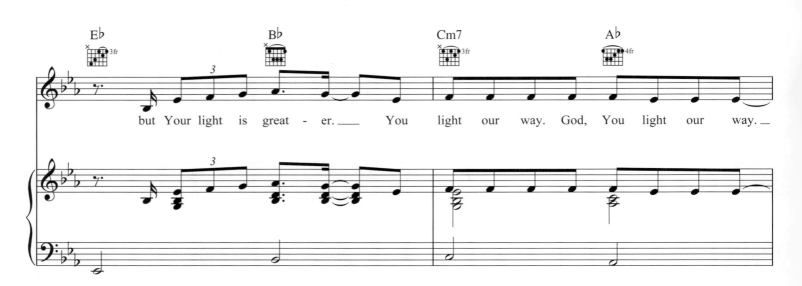

Death had a strong - hold, __ but Your life was strong - er. __ Rose

from the grave, rose up from the grave. __ When e - vil is ris - ing, __

You're ris - ing high - er __ with pow'r to save, with pow - er to save. __

__ You keep hope a - live, You keep hope a - live.

START RIGHT HERE

Words and Music by MATTHEW WEST,
BERNIE HERMS, MARK HALL
and SETH MOSLEY

chest.

He did-n't run ___ off ___ like his broth - er, ___

but his soul was just as dead.

What if the church on

Sun - day ___ was still the church on ___ Mon - day,

too?

What if we came down ___ from our